THE FREEDOM FORMULA

How to Create Passive Income

and Live Life on Your Own Terms

By Ashley Layna

INTRODUCTION

Are you tired of living paycheck to paycheck, working long hours, and feeling like you're not making any progress towards your financial goals?

If so, you're not alone. Many people are looking for a better way to earn money and live a more fulfilling life. The good news is that it's possible to create a sustainable income stream without working harder or sacrificing your time and energy.

In this ebook, we'll explore the concept of passive income and how it can help you achieve your financial goals and live life on your own terms. We'll cover a variety of passive income streams, including real estate investing, dividend stocks, online businesses, and more. We'll also provide practical tips and strategies for building and managing passive income streams, as well as advice on how to avoid common pitfalls and maximize your earnings.

Whether you're looking to supplement your current income, build long-term wealth, or simply enjoy more free time, this ebook will provide you with the knowledge and tools you need to achieve your goals. So sit back, relax, and let's explore the exciting world of passive income together.

CONTENTS

OVERVIEW

AFFILIATE MARKETING

Definition of passive income

Definition of affiliate marketing

The benefits of generating passive income

Benefits of affiliate marketing

Overview of the different types of passive income streams How to choose affiliate products and programs Risks and challenges of affiliate marketing Tips for successful affiliate marketing

REAL ESTATE INVESTING

PEER-TO-PEER LENDING

Benefits of investing in real estate

Definition of peer-to-peer lending

Types of real estate investments (rental properties, flipping houses,
Benefits of peer-to-peer lending

REITs, crowdfunding)

How to choose a peer-to-peer lending platform Risks and
challenges of real estate investing Risks and challenges of peer-to-
peer lending Tips for successful real estate investing

Tips for successful peer-to-peer lending

DIVIDEND INVESTING

CREATING A RENTAL BUSINESS

Definition of dividend investing

Overview of creating a rental business

Benefits of dividend investing

Benefits of creating a rental business

How to choose dividend stocks

Types of rental businesses (equipment rental, vacation rental, car
Risks and challenges of dividend investing

rental, etc.)

Tips for successful dividend investing

Risks and challenges of creating a rental business Tips for
successful rental business creation and management CREATING
& SELLING DIGITAL PRODUCTS

CONCLUSION

Overview of digital products (e-books, online courses, software, Recap of the benefits of generating passive income etc.)

Final thoughts on achieving financial independence through Benefits of creating and selling digital products passive income

How to create and market digital products

Call to action for readers to start building their passive income Risks and challenges of creating and selling digital products streams.

Tips for successful digital product creation and sales

OVERVIEW

What is passive income?

Passive income is income that is earned without requiring active involvement or ongoing effort.

In other words, it's money that is generated with minimal work or time investment on an ongoing basis.

Passive income is often contrasted with active income, which is earned through direct work or labor, such as a salary from a job. While active income can be a reliable source of income, it typically requires ongoing work and effort to maintain.

Passive income can come from a variety of sources, such as rental properties, dividend stocks, online businesses, and more. The key characteristic of passive income is that it continues to generate income over time, even if you're not actively working on it.

Generating passive income can be a powerful way to achieve financial independence and create more freedom and flexibility in your life. However, it's important to note that creating passive income streams often requires upfront investment and effort, such as investing in real estate or creating a digital product. It's also important to carefully research and understand the risks and potential rewards of any passive income opportunity before investing time or money into it.

Real Estate Investing ~ Dividend Investing

Selling Digital Products ~ Affiliate Marketing Peer-to-peer lending ~ Rental Business

"If you don't find a

way to make money

while you sleep, you

will work until you die."

~ Warren Buffett

REAL ESTATE

Benefits of Investing

in Real Estate

One of the main benefits of investing in real estate is the potential for passive income. Rental properties, for example, can generate consistent monthly income from rental payments. This income can provide a steady stream of cash flow that can help investors achieve financial goals such as retirement, paying off debt, or saving for other investments.

Real estate investments also have the potential for long-term appreciation. Over time, properties tend to increase in value, especially in desirable locations. This appreciation can provide a significant return on investment when the property is eventually sold, making it a valuable asset in a well-diversified investment portfolio.

Real estate investments also offer many tax advantages.

For example, rental income is generally considered passive income and is subject to different tax rules than earned income. Additionally, investors can take Real estate investments also offer

advantage of deducting expenses related to their real estate investments, such as property taxes, mortgage investors a high degree of control over

interest, and property management fees. These tax their investments. Unlike other

advantages can help investors reduce their taxable investments that are subject to market

income and keep more of their profits.

fluctuations, real estate investors can

make improvements to their properties,

Real estate investments can also provide diversification to an investment portfolio. Real estate is a physical raise rents, and make other changes to asset that can hold value even in times of economic increase the value of their investments.

uncertainty. This can help investors reduce their overall This level of control can provide investors portfolio risk and provide a hedge against inflation.

Additionally, real estate investments can be less volatile with a greater sense of security and the

than other investments, such as stocks and bonds, ability to make strategic decisions to

providing a stable source of income.

maximize their returns.

Overall, investing in real estate can

provide many benefits, including

potential for passive income, long-term

appreciation, tax advantages,

diversification, and control. However, it's important to carefully research and

understand the risks and potential

rewards of any real estate investment

before investing time or money into it.

"9

" 0

9 %

0

% of

o fal

a ll lmi

m lillilo

i n

o a

n i

a r

i e

r s

e

be

b c

e o

c m

o e

m eso

s

o th

t r

h o

r u

o g

u h

g

ow

o n

w i

n n

i g

n

g re

r a

e l

a les

e t

s a

t t

a e

t .

e "

.

~

~ An

A d

n r

d e

r w

e

w Ca

C r

a n

r e

n g

e i

g e

i

REAL ESTATE

Types of Real Estate

Crowdfunding: Crowdfunding platforms allow investors to pool
Investing

their money together to invest in real estate properties. This can
include both debt and equity investments, depending on the Rental
properties involve purchasing a property and then platform and the
investment opportunity. Crowdfunding can renting it out to tenants
for monthly rent payments. This provide access to real estate
investments that may not be available to individual investors, as
well as potential for passive income and can include single-family
homes, multi-unit apartment diversification. However,
crowdfunding investments are often buildings, or commercial
properties. Rental properties can illiquid and may not provide the
same level of control and provide a steady source of passive
income for investors, as transparency as other types of
investments.

well as long-term appreciation and tax advantages.

However, rental properties also require ongoing Real Estate Syndication: Real estate syndication involves pooling management and maintenance, as well as dealing with together resources from multiple investors to purchase and manage potential tenant issues.

a property or portfolio of properties. This can include both debt and equity investments, depending on the structure of the Rental properties involve purchasing a property and then syndication. Real estate syndication can provide access to larger and more complex investment opportunities, as well as potential renting it out to tenants for monthly rent payments. This for passive income and diversification. However, real estate can include single-family homes, multi-unit apartment syndication requires a high level of trust among the investors and buildings, or commercial properties. Rental properties can the syndicator, as well as careful due diligence and legal provide a steady source of passive income for investors, as compliance.

well as long-term appreciation and tax advantages.

However, rental properties also require ongoing Overall, there are many different types of real estate investments management and maintenance, as well as dealing with available to investors, each with its own benefits and risks. Before potential tenant issues.

investing in real estate, it's important to carefully research and understand the options and to have a clear investment strategy in place. This can help investors maximize their returns and achieve Real Estate Investment Trusts (REITs): REITs are their financial goals.

companies that own and manage income-producing real estate properties, such as apartment complexes or office buildings. Investors can purchase shares in a REIT, which

"R

" e

R a

e l

a les

e t

s a

t t

a e

t ein

i v

n e

v s

e t

s i

t n

i g

n ,

g ,ev

e e

v n

e

n on

o

n a

provides them with the potential for passive income *ve*

v r

e y

r

y sm

s a

m l

a ll lsc

s a

c l

a e

l ,

e ,re

r m

e a

m i

a n

i s

n sa

a tr

t i

r e

i d

e

without the need to manage the properties themselves.
REITs can provide diversification to an investment *an*

a d

n

d tr

t u

r e

u eme

m a

e n

a s

n sof

o fbu

b i

u lid

l i

d n

i g

n

g an

a

portfolio, as well as liquidity and transparency. However, *in*

i d

n i

d v

i i

v d

i u

d a

u l

a 'ls

' sca

c s

a h

s

h flfo

l w

o

w an

a d

n

REITs are subject to market volatility and management *we*

w a

e l

a tlh

t .

h "

.

fees.

~

~ Ro

R b

o e

b r

e t

r tKi

K y

i o

y s

o a

s k

a i

k

REAL ESTATE

Risks & Chal enges

One of the biggest challenges of real estate investing is the significant amount of upfront capital required to purchase a property. This can limit access to real estate investments for many investors, especially those without significant savings or access to financing. Additionally, real estate investments can be illiquid, meaning it's difficult to quickly sell or liquidate the investment if needed.

Real estate investments also require ongoing management and maintenance, which can be time-consuming and costly. This can include finding and managing tenants, handling repairs and maintenance, and dealing with unexpected issues that may arise. If an investor is unable or unwilling to manage the property themselves, they may need to pay for property management services, which can cut into profits.

Real estate investments are also subject to market fluctuations and changes in the local housing market.

Economic downturns or changes in interest rates can impact the value of a property, as well as the demand for rental properties. This can make real estate investments more volatile than other types of investments, such as stocks or bonds.

Real estate investments can also be subject to unexpected expenses, such as repairs from natural disasters or tenant damage. These expenses can eat into profits and impact the overall return on investment.

Additionally, real estate investments may require ongoing upgrades and improvements to maintain their value over time.

Real estate investments are also subject to a variety of legal and regulatory issues, including zoning laws, building codes, and landlord-tenant laws. Failure to comply with these laws and regulations can result in

"A ship is safe in harbor, but

fines and legal issues, which can impact the overall profitability of the investment.

that's not what ships are

Overall, real estate investing can be a challenging and for."

risky endeavor that requires significant upfront capital, ongoing management and maintenance, and the

~ William Shedd

potential for unexpected expenses and market fluctuations. However, with careful research and planning, real estate investments can provide a steady source of passive income and long-term appreciation, making them a valuable asset in a well-diversified investment portfolio.

"Success is not final, failure REAL ESTATE

is not fatal: It is the courage

Tips for Succes ful

to continue that counts."

Real Estate Investing

~ Winston Churchill.

Do your research: Before investing in real estate, it's important to do your research. This Be patient: Real estate investing is a long-term includes understanding the local real estate game, so it's important to be patient. Don't market, analyzing property values and rental expect to make a quick profit overnight.

rates,

and

researching

potential

Instead, focus on building a diversified neighborhoods. You should also stay up-to-portfolio of properties that will generate steady date on real estate trends, laws, and income over time. Be prepared to weather regulations that could impact your investment.

market fluctuations and be willing to adapt your strategy as needed. With patience and Create a plan: Once you've done your persistence, real estate investing can be a research, create a solid investment plan. This lucrative and rewarding venture.

should include your investment goals, budget, and timeline. Think about what kind of In conclusion, successful real estate investing properties you want to invest in (e.g.

requires careful research, planning, and residential, commercial, multi-family), and financial management. It's important to consider the risks and benefits of each. Having understand the local real estate market, create a clear plan in place will help you stay focused a solid investment plan, build a team of and make informed decisions.

professionals, manage your finances wisely, and be patient for long-term success. By following Build a team: Successful real estate investing these tips, you'll be able to make informed often requires a team of professionals, such as decisions and build a diversified portfolio of a real estate agent, attorney, accountant, and properties that can generate steady income property manager. These individuals can help over time. Remember, real estate investing you navigate the complex world of real estate requires a long-term mindset and a willingness and provide valuable guidance and advice. Be to adapt to changing market conditions. With sure to choose professionals that have the right approach, real estate investing can experience in the specific type of real estate offer a lucrative and rewarding opportunity for you're investing in.

investors.

Manage your finances wisely: Real estate In conclusion, successful real estate investing investing can be expensive, so it's important to requires careful research, planning, and manage your finances wisely. This includes financial management. It's important to creating a budget, securing financing, and understand the local real estate market, create keeping track of expenses. You should also a solid investment plan, build a team of consider the potential return on investment professionals, manage your finances wisely, and (ROI) of each property before making a be patient for long-term success.

purchase.

DIVDEND INVESTING

Mutual funds and ETFs can also be dividend products.

What is Divdend Ivesting

These investments are typically made up of a portfolio of individual stocks or other securities, with the dividends from these underlying holdings passed through to the fund's shareholders. Some mutual funds and ETFs are specifically focused on dividend-paying stocks, while others may have a mix of dividend and Dividend products are investments that pay out non-dividend paying investments.

regular dividends to their shareholders. Dividends are a portion of a company's profits that are distributed to Dividend products can be an attractive option for shareholders as a way to provide a return on their income-seeking investors, as they can provide a regular investment. Dividend products can include stocks, stream of cash flow without requiring the investor to mutual funds, exchange-traded funds (ETFs), and sell shares of the investment. However, it's important to other types of investments.

note that dividend payments are not guaranteed and can be reduced or eliminated if a company's profits Dividend stocks are typically issued by established decline. Investors should also be aware of the tax companies with a track record of consistent profits and implications of dividend income, as it is typically taxed dividend payments. These companies tend to be less at a different rate than capital gains.

volatile than newer or smaller companies, making In summary, dividend products are investments that pay out them a popular choice for investors seeking a steady regular dividends to their shareholders. These products can include stocks, mutual funds, ETFs, and other types of stream of income. Dividend stocks can be either investments. Dividend products can provide a steady stream of common or preferred shares, with preferred shares income for investors, but it's important to carefully consider typically paying a higher dividend rate but carrying the risks and tax implications before making any investment less voting power.

decisions.

"Rule No. 1: Never lose money. Rule No. 2: Never forget rule No.1." - Warren Buffett.

"Dividends aren't the only thing, they're everything."

~ James P. O'Shaughnessy.

DIVIDEND INVESTING

Benefits of Dividend Investing

Steady Income: One of the most significant benefits of dividend investing is that it provides a steady stream of income. Dividend-paying stocks are companies that share their profits with shareholders in the form of dividends. These payments can provide a reliable source of income for investors, making them an attractive investment option for those looking for a regular income stream.

Compounding Returns: Another benefit of dividend investing is the power of compounding returns. When investors reinvest their dividends, they purchase additional shares of the company, which can lead to increased dividend payments in the future. Over time, this can result in significant growth in the value of an investor's portfolio.

Lower Risk: Companies that pay dividends tend to be Historically, dividend-well-established, financially stable businesses with a

long track record of profitability. This makes them less risky
paying stocks have

than companies that do not pay dividends as they are less likely to
experience significant fluctuations in their outperformed non-stock
price. Additionally, dividend-paying companies dividend-paying
stocks

have historically outperformed non-dividend-paying companies
over the long term, providing investors with a over the long term.

measure of downside protection.

Inflation Hedge: Dividend-paying stocks can also provide an
inflation hedge for investors. As the cost of living increases, so do
dividend payments. This means that investors who hold dividend-
paying stocks can potentially keep pace with inflation and
maintain the purchasing power of their income stream.

Tax Advantages: Finally, dividend investing can offer tax
advantages for investors. In many countries, including the United
States, qualified dividends are taxed at a lower rate than ordinary
income. This can result in significant tax savings for investors,
allowing them to keep more of their income and reinvest it back
into their portfolios.

Overall, dividend investing can provide investors with a number of
benefits, including a steady income stream, compounding returns,
lower risk, an inflation hedge, and tax advantages. While dividend
investing may not be suitable for all investors, those looking for a
reliable source of income and long-term growth may find it to be a
valuable addition to their investment portfolio.

DIVIDEND INVESTING

How to Choose Dividend Stocks

Look for established companies. One of the first things to consider when choosing dividend stocks is the stability and financial strength of the company. Look for companies with a long history of profitability, a solid balance sheet, and a sustainable business model. Established companies with a track record of success are more likely to be able to continue paying dividends even in challenging economic conditions.

Evaluate the dividend yield. The dividend yield is the annual dividend payment divided by the current stock price, expressed as a percentage. A higher dividend yield can be attractive to investors looking for income, but it's important to remember that a high yield can also be a red flag. A dividend yield that is significantly higher than the average for the sector or the market as a whole may indicate that the company is struggling or that the dividend is not sustainable.

The payout ratio is the percentage of earnings that are paid out as dividends. A low payout ratio indicates that the company is retaining a significant portion of its earnings for future growth, while a high payout ratio may indicate that the company is paying out more than it can afford. Look for companies with a payout ratio that is sustainable and in line with the industry average.

SConsider dividend growth: Another important factor to consider when choosing dividend stocks is the company's track record of dividend growth. Companies that consistently increase their dividends over time can provide investors with a growing income stream and can also be an indication of a healthy business. Look for companies with a history of steady and sustainable dividend growth.

Evaluate the company's prospects: Finally, it's important to consider the company's prospects for future growth and profitability. Look for companies with a strong competitive position in their industry, a solid growth strategy, and a history of investing in research and development. Companies that are well-positioned for future growth are more likely to be able to continue paying dividends and may also provide investors with long-term capital appreciation.

Overall, when choosing dividend stocks, investors should consider factors such as the stability and financial strength of the company, the dividend yield, the payout ratio, the track record of dividend growth, and the company's prospects for future growth and profitability. By taking a comprehensive approach to selecting dividend stocks, investors can potentially build a portfolio of high-quality companies that can provide both income and long-term growth.

DIVIDEND

Tips for Succes ful Dividend

INVESTING

Investing

One of the most important tips for successful It's important to regularly monitor your dividend-dividend investing is to diversify your portfolio.

paying stocks to ensure that the companies are This means investing in a variety of dividend-continuing to perform well and that the dividends paying stocks across different sectors and

are sustainable. Keep an eye on the company's industries to reduce the risk of concentrated financial statements, earnings reports, and other exposure to any one company or sector.

relevant news to stay informed about any changes Diversification can help ensure that your portfolio that could impact the dividend payment.

is well-positioned to weather market volatility and economic downturns.

Be patient: Finally, successful dividend investing requires patience. Dividend investing is a long-Another important tip for successful dividend term strategy, and it may take time for your investing is to reinvest your dividends. By investments to generate significant returns. It's reinvesting your dividends, you can purchase important to have a long-term perspective and to additional shares of the company, which can lead resist the temptation to make frequent trades to increased dividend payments in the future.

based on short-term market fluctuations.

Over time, this can result in significant growth in the value of your portfolio, as well as a growing Overall, successful dividend investing requires a income stream.

diversified portfolio, a focus on quality, regular monitoring of your holdings, and a long-term When selecting dividend-paying stocks, it's perspective. By following these tips, investors can important to focus on quality. Look for potentially build a portfolio of high-quality companies with a long history of profitability, a dividend-paying stocks that can provide both solid balance sheet, and a sustainable business income and long-term growth.

model. Companies that are financially stable and well-positioned for future growth are more likely to be able to continue paying dividends over the long term.

CREATING & SELLING

DIGITAL PRODUCTS

Overview

Digital products are any products that can be Once the digital product is developed, it can be delivered electronically, such as software, ebooks, sold through a variety of channels. Online music, videos, and courses. Creating and selling marketplaces like Amazon, Etsy, or Udemy digital products involves developing a product in provide a platform for creators to sell their digital a digital format and making it available for products to a large audience. Alternatively, purchase or download through an online platform.

creators can sell their products directly through Digital products can be created by individuals, their

own

website,

using

tools

like

small businesses, or large corporations, and can be WooCommerce or Shopify to set up an online sold through a variety of online marketplaces or store and process payments.

through a company's own website.

To be successful at creating and selling digital To create a digital product, it's important to have products, it's important to have a clear a clear idea of the product's purpose, target understanding of the target audience, to develop a audience, and features. This may involve high-quality product that meets their needs, and conducting market research, brainstorming ideas, to market the product effectively. This may and developing a detailed plan for the product's involve building an online presence through social development. Depending on the type of digital media, email marketing, or content marketing, product, this may involve coding, designing, and using paid advertising to reach a wider writing, or recording.

audience. By creating a high-quality digital product and effectively promoting it to the right audience, creators can generate a profitable source of income and build a successful online business.

CREATING & SELLING

DIGITAL PRODUCTS

Benefits of Creating & Sel ing

Digital Products

Scalability: One of the key benefits of creating and selling digital products is the scalability of the business model. Unlike physical products, digital products can be easily replicated and sold an unlimited number of times, without the need for additional manufacturing or shipping costs. This means that creators can potentially generate a significant amount of revenue from a single digital product, and can easily scale their business by creating and selling additional digital products.

Low overhead costs: Another benefit of creating and selling digital products is the low overhead costs. Since digital products can be created and distributed electronically, there are no

manufacturing or shipping costs, and creators can operate their business from anywhere with an internet connection. This makes digital product creation an attractive option for individuals and small businesses looking to start a business without significant upfront costs.

Global reach: Digital products can be sold

globally, without the need for physical

distribution channels. This means that creators can potentially reach a much larger audience than with physical products, and can sell their products to customers all over the world. This can result in increased revenue and a more diverse customer base.

Passive income: Digital products can also provide a source of passive income, meaning that creators can continue to generate revenue from their products long after they have been created. This is particularly true for evergreen digital products, such as ebooks or online courses, that continue to be in demand over time. This can provide creators with a steady stream of income and the flexibility to focus on other projects or activities.

Creative freedom: Finally, creating and selling digital products provides creators with a high degree of creative freedom. Since digital products can take many forms, from ebooks to online

courses to software, creators have the ability to develop products that align with their interests, skills, and expertise. This can result in a more fulfilling and enjoyable work experience, as well as the potential for

increased revenue and business success.

CREATING & SELLING

DIGITAL PRODUCTS

How to Create & Market

Digital Products

The first step in creating and marketing a digital product is to choose a niche or area of expertise. This could be a specific topic or problem that you have knowledge and experience in, or a gap in the market that you have identified. By choosing a niche, you can focus your product development and marketing efforts on a specific audience, which can increase your chances of success.

Once you have chosen a niche, the next step is to develop your digital product. This may involve creating written content like ebooks or blog posts, producing video or audio content like courses or podcasts, or developing software or apps. When developing your product, it's important to keep your target audience in mind and to create content that is valuable, engaging, and solves a specific problem or meets a specific need.

To market your digital product, you'll need a website or landing page where you can showcase your product and collect leads or sales. This may involve building a website using a platform like WordPress or Squarespace, or using a landing page builder like Leadpages or ClickFunnels. You'll also need to develop a sales funnel, which is a series of steps that guide potential customers from awareness to purchase, such as offering a free lead magnet, providing value through email marketing, and eventually offering your product for sale.

Once you have developed your product and built your website and sales funnel, the next step is to promote your product. This may involve using a variety of marketing strategies, such as content marketing, social media marketing, paid advertising, or influencer marketing. It's important to choose marketing channels that align with your target audience and to track your results to see which strategies are most effective.

Finally, to create a successful digital product and build a loyal customer base, it's important to provide excellent customer service. This may involve offering timely support and assistance to customers who have questions or issues, providing regular updates and improvements to your product, and actively engaging with your customers through social media or email marketing. By building strong relationships with your customers, you can generate positive reviews and word-of-mouth referrals, which can help to drive further sales and growth.

Overall, creating and marketing a digital product requires careful planning, development, and promotion.

By following these steps and focusing on providing value to your target audience, you can create a successful digital product and build a profitable online business.

CREATING & SELLING

DIGITAL PRODUCTS

Risks & Chal enges

One of the biggest risks of creating and selling digital products is the risk of intellectual property infringement. This can occur if you unknowingly use copyrighted material in your product, or if someone else copies or steals your product and sells it as their own. To mitigate this risk, it's important to conduct thorough research and

ensure that you have the necessary licenses and permissions to use any third-party material, as well as to take steps to protect your own intellectual property, such as trademarking your brand and copyrighting your content.

Another challenge of creating and selling digital products is the risk of market saturation. With so many digital products available online, it can be difficult to differentiate yourself from the competition and attract customers. To overcome this challenge, it's important to focus on creating high-quality, valuable content that meets a specific need or solves a specific problem, as well as to develop a strong brand and marketing strategy that resonates with your target audience.

Another challenge of selling digital products is the risk of payment processing issues, such as credit Creating and selling digital products also card fraud or chargebacks. To minimize this risk, comes with the risk of technical issues, such it's important to use a secure payment processing as glitches or bugs in software or system and to implement fraud prevention measures, such as requiring a CVV code or limiting compatibility issues with different devices. the number of transactions per customer.

To mitigate this risk, it's important to thoroughly test your product before release, Finally, creating and selling digital products can as well as to provide clear instructions and also be challenging when it comes to providing troubleshooting resources for customers who customer support. Unlike physical products, digital may encounter technical issues.

products can be difficult to troubleshoot or provide assistance with remotely. To overcome this challenge, it's important to provide clear and detailed instructions for using your product, as well as to offer prompt and responsive customer support through channels like email, chat, or phone.

CREATING & SELLING DIGITAL PRODUCTS

Tips for Succes

Focus on your audience: To create a successful digital product, it's important to focus on your target audience and create content that meets their specific needs or solves their specific problems. This may involve conducting market research, surveying your audience, or analyzing their feedback to identify areas where you can provide value. By understanding your audience and creating content that resonates with them, you can increase the chances of your product being successful.

Provide value: Another key aspect of successful digital product creation and sales is providing value to your customers. This may involve offering high-quality content, useful tools or resources, or personalized coaching or support.

By providing value to your customers, you can build trust and credibility, which can lead to increased sales and customer loyalty.

Offer a clear value proposition: To sell your digital product effectively, it's important to offer a clear value proposition that explains what your product is, how it works, and what benefits it provides. This may involve creating a sales page or landing page that highlights the features and benefits of your product, as well as using persuasive language and visual elements to engage your audience and encourage them to Continuously improve: Finally, to create and sell successful digital products, it's important to take action.

continuously improve and update your content, based on feedback from your audience and changes in the market.

Invest in marketing: Successful digital product This may involve conducting regular surveys or polls, creation and sales also requires effective analyzing website analytics or sales data, or marketing. This may involve using a variety of experimenting with new features or formats. By strategies, such as content marketing, social continuously improving and refining your digital media marketing, email marketing, paid

products, you can stay ahead of the competition and advertising, or influencer marketing. It's provide ongoing value to your customers.

important to choose marketing channels that Overall, creating and selling successful digital products align with your target audience and to track requires a combination of effective marketing, audience your results to see which strategies are most research, value proposition development, and ongoing effective.

improvement. By following these tips and focusing on providing value to your customers, you can build a profitable and sustainable online business.

AFFILIATE MARKETING

What is Affiliate Marketing

Affiliate marketing is a type of performance-based To participate in affiliate marketing, companies marketing in which a company or individual pays a typically join an affiliate network or program, which commission to affiliates for promoting their products provides a platform for them to track and manage or services. Affiliates are typically individuals or their affiliate relationships. Affiliates can then sign businesses who promote the products or services of up to promote the company's products or services the company in exchange for a commission on any and receive a unique affiliate link or code, which they resulting sales or leads. This can be done through can use to track their sales or referrals. The company various channels, such as a website, social media, typically provides marketing materials, such as email marketing, or paid advertising.

banners, ads, or email templates, to help affiliates promote their products or services effectively.

Affiliate marketing is based on the concept of revenue sharing, in which the company rewards its Overall, affiliate marketing is a popular and effective affiliates for the sales or leads they generate. This way for companies to expand their reach and increase creates a win-win situation, as the company benefits their sales, while providing affiliates with an from increased exposure and sales, while the affiliates opportunity to earn a commission for promoting earn a commission for promoting the products or products or services they believe in. By developing services. Affiliate marketing can be a cost-effective strong relationships with affiliates and providing way for companies to expand their reach and increase them with the tools and resources they need to their sales, as they only pay commissions on actual succeed, companies can build a thriving affiliate results.

marketing program and drive sustainable growth.

AFFILIATE MARKETING

Benefits of Affiliate Marketing

Affiliate marketing offers significant revenue potential for individuals and businesses. As an affiliate marketer, you can earn commissions for promoting and selling products or services on behalf of other companies. With the right strategies and targeted marketing efforts, you can generate passive income streams and scale your earnings.

Unlike traditional business models, affiliate marketing allows you to earn money without the need to create or maintain your own products.

One of the advantages of affiliate marketing is its low barrier to entry. You don't need to invest substantial capital to get started. There are no costs associated with product creation, inventory management, or order fulfillment. The primary investment is your time and effort in building an online presence, creating engaging content, and driving traffic to affiliate offers. This makes it an accessible business model for aspiring entrepreneurs, bloggers, or content creators looking to monetize their platforms.

Affiliate marketing provides a high degree of flexibility and location independence. You can work from anywhere with an internet connection, allowing you to create a lifestyle that suits your preferences. Whether you prefer working from home, traveling, or being a digital nomad, affiliate marketing offers the freedom to set your own schedule and work at your own pace. This

flexibility also enables you to pursue other interests or maintain a work-life balance while still earning income from your affiliate marketing efforts.

"Success is not the key to

Affiliate marketing presents a compelling

opportunity for individuals and businesses to earn happiness. Happiness is the

income by promoting products or services. Its key to success. If you love

revenue potential, low startup costs, flexibility, and wide range of products to choose from make it an what you are doing, you will

attractive option for those seeking to monetize their online presence and build sustainable income be successful."

streams.

~Albert Schweitzer

AFFILIATE MARKETING

"Choose your affiliations

wisely, for they shape your

How to Choose Affiliate

path to success." ~Unknown

Products & Programso

When selecting affiliate products, it's crucial to When evaluating affiliate programs, consider the research and evaluate them thoroughly. Consider program's conversion rates and cookie duration.

the quality, relevance, and value the product or Conversion rates refer to the percentage of visitors service offers to your target audience. Assess its who make a purchase after clicking on your affiliate reputation, customer reviews, and overall demand link. Look for programs with higher conversion in the market. Look for products that align with rates as it indicates that the product or service has a your niche and have a proven track record of strong appeal and is more likely to convert your customer satisfaction. It's also important to ensure referrals into sales. Additionally, pay attention to that the product or service complements your the cookie duration, which determines how long content and resonates with your audience's needs you will receive credit for a referral's purchase.

and interests.

Longer cookie durations provide a higher chance of earning commissions if a customer makes a Examine the commission structure and earnings purchase within the specified timeframe.

potential of the affiliate program. Evaluate the commission rates, whether they are fixed or tiered, Reliable tracking and timely payments are essential and how they compare to similar products or aspects of a good affiliate program. Ensure that the programs in the market. Additionally, consider the program has robust tracking systems in place to average order value and the potential for recurring accurately record and attribute sales generated commissions if the product has a subscription or through your referrals. This ensures that you membership model. Aim for affiliate programs that receive proper credit and commissions for your offer fair and competitive commission rates, efforts. Additionally, look for programs that have a allowing you to earn a reasonable income for your reputation for timely and consistent payments.

promotional efforts.

Prompt payment cycles indicate that the program is reliable and committed to supporting their It's crucial to review the affiliate program's affiliates. Reliable tracking and timely payments policies, terms, and conditions. Look for contribute to a positive and trustworthy partnership transparency, clear guidelines, and fair practices.

with the affiliate program.

Assess how the program tracks and reports sales, as accurate tracking is essential for ensuring you By considering the affiliate program's conversion receive proper credit for your referrals.

rates, cookie duration, tracking reliability, and Additionally, consider the level of support and payment practices, you can choose programs that resources provided by the program. Look for maximize your earnings potential and provide a programs that offer marketing materials, training seamless experience for both you and your resources, and dedicated affiliate support to assist audience. Keep in mind that selecting the right you in your promotional efforts and maximize your affiliate products and programs is an ongoing chances of success.

process, and it's important to regularly assess their performance, adapt to market trends, and make adjustments as necessary to optimize your affiliate marketing efforts.

AFFILIATE MARKETING

Risks & Chal enges

The popularity of affiliate marketing has led to increased competition and saturation in many niches. It can be One of the risks in affiliate marketing is the potential challenging to stand out among other affiliates promoting the for commission reductions or program terminations.

same or similar products. Building a unique brand, providing Affiliate programs may change their commission value through high-quality content, and establishing strong structure, lower commission rates, or even terminate relationships with your audience can help differentiate you from competitors. It's important to continuously refine your their program altogether. This can significantly impact marketing tactics, explore untapped niches, and seek your earnings and disrupt your income stream. It's innovative approaches to maintain a competitive edge in the important to stay informed about any program updates crowded affiliate marketing landscape.

and be prepared to adapt your marketing strategies or seek alternative affiliate partnerships to mitigate the Affiliate marketing involves promoting and endorsing risks associated with program changes.

products or services. It's crucial to adhere to ethical practices and comply with applicable laws and regulations, such as Affiliate marketing relies on external factors beyond disclosing affiliate relationships, providing accurate information, and avoiding deceptive marketing tactics. Failure your control, such as changes in market trends, to meet ethical and legal standards can lead to reputational product availability, or consumer preferences.

damage, legal consequences, or account suspension from Fluctuations in the market, economic conditions, or affiliate networks. Being mindful of ethical guidelines and shifts in consumer behavior can affect the demand for staying updated on relevant regulations is essential to maintain certain products or services, which, in turn, impacts a trustworthy and sustainable affiliate marketing business.

your potential to earn commissions. To navigate this challenge, it's crucial to diversify your affiliate Despite the risks and challenges, affiliate marketing remains a portfolio, promote a range of products across different viable and potentially lucrative business model. By staying proactive, adapting to changes, diversifying your affiliate niches, and stay informed about industry trends to portfolio, and adhering to ethical practices, you can navigate adapt your marketing strategies accordingly.

these challenges and build a successful affiliate marketing venture.

"Success in affiliate marketing requires adaptability, resilience, and an unwavering commitment to ethical practices." - Unknown

AFFILIATE MARKETING

Tips for Succes

One of the key tips for success in affiliate marketing is to deeply understand your target audience. Take the time to research and analyze their demographics, interests, needs, and pain points. By gaining a comprehensive understanding of your audience, you can tailor your content, promotions, and product recommendations to resonate with them effectively.

Engage with your audience through social media, email marketing, or blog comments to gather feedback and insights that can inform your affiliate marketing strategies. By providing valuable and relevant content that addresses their specific needs, you can build trust, credibility, and loyalty, leading to higher conversion rates and long-term success.

Selecting high-quality products and services to promote is crucial for success in affiliate marketing.

Ensure that the products align with your niche and offer value to your audience. Conduct thorough research to assess the reputation, reliability, and customer satisfaction associated with the products or services you plan to promote. By recommending products that are reputable, reliable, and of high quality, you enhance your credibility as an affiliate marketer and increase the likelihood of generating conversions. Choose affiliate programs that have a strong track record, provide adequate support, and offer competitive commission rates to ensure a mutually beneficial partnership.

Building trust and authenticity is paramount in affiliate marketing. Focus on creating genuine and Success in affiliate marketing relies on staying valuable content that educates, informs, and inspires ahead of the curve and adapting to industry your audience. Be transparent about your affiliate changes. Stay updated on the latest trends, relationships and disclose any potential biases or conflicts of interest. Honesty and transparency foster technologies, and marketing strategies relevant to trust with your audience, and they appreciate affiliate marketing. Invest time in ongoing authenticity in recommendations. Avoid excessive education, attend industry conferences, and follow promotion or endorsing products solely for the sake thought leaders in the field. Experiment with of earning commissions. Instead, provide balanced different promotional tactics, track your results, and

unbiased

reviews,

showcase

personal

and optimize your approach based on data and experiences, and offer honest recommendations insights. Embrace a growth mindset and be open to based on your expertise and understanding of your testing new ideas and approaches. By continuously audience's needs. By consistently delivering value learning, refining your strategies, and staying agile, and demonstrating your integrity, you can build a loyal following and drive sustainable success in you can stay competitive in the ever-evolving affiliate marketing.

landscape of affiliate marketing and maximize your earning potential.

PEER-TO-PEER LENDING

What is Pe r-to-Pe r Lending?

Peer-to-peer lending, also known as P2P lending or social Peer-to-peer lending offers several benefits for both lending, is a form of lending that connects individuals or borrowers and lenders. For borrowers, P2P lending can

"peers" who are looking to borrow money with individuals provide faster loan approval, more flexible terms, and or investors willing to lend money. It bypasses traditional potentially lower interest rates compared to traditional financial intermediaries such as banks or credit unions and lenders. Additionally, individuals with less-than-perfect operates through online platforms that facilitate the credit histories or limited access to traditional financial lending process. P2P lending platforms act as institutions may find it easier to secure funding through intermediaries, matching borrowers and lenders, and P2P lending platforms. For lenders, P2P lending offers the providing the necessary infrastructure to facilitate loan opportunity to earn potentially higher returns compared to transactions. The lending process typically involves traditional savings or investment options. Lenders can borrowers creating loan listings stating the desired loan diversify their investment portfolio by spreading their funds amount and purpose, while lenders assess these listings and across multiple loans and borrowers, mitigating risks.

decide which loans to fund based on their risk appetite and However, it's important to note that peer-to-peer lending interest rate expectations.

carries certain risks, including the possibility of borrower default or late payments, lack of collateral, and the Peer-to-peer lending platforms provide borrowers with an potential for platform risk or fraud. Lenders should alternative source of financing compared to traditional carefully assess the creditworthiness of borrowers and loans. Borrowers can access funds for various purposes, consider the associated risks before participating in P2P

such as debt consolidation, small business loans, education lending activities.

expenses, or personal needs. The loan application process is typically streamlined and conducted online, allowing Peer-to-peer lending has gained popularity as an alternative borrowers to submit their loan requests and relevant lending option, leveraging technology and connectivity to documentation for review. Once approved, the loans are facilitate direct transactions between borrowers and funded by individual lenders who contribute small portions lenders. It provides a decentralized approach to financing of the total loan amount. As the loan is repaid, the monthly and offers opportunities for individuals to access funds or payments are distributed among the lenders, with interest, invest their money outside of traditional banking channels.

according to their respective investment amounts.

PEER-TO-PEER LENDING

"According to a recent study, the global peer-to-peer lending market is projected to reach a value of $558.91 billion by 2027, showcasing Benefits of Pe r-to-Pe r

the tremendous growth and potential of this alternative lending model."

Lending

Peer-to-peer lending provides individuals and small Peer-to-peer lending platforms often offer a streamlined businesses with an alternative source of financing.

and user-friendly application and approval process.

Traditional lenders often have stringent criteria, making Borrowers can easily create loan listings, provide it challenging for certain borrowers to secure loans.

necessary documentation, and submit their loan requests Peer-to-peer lending platforms offer a more inclusive online. This eliminates the need for extensive paperwork approach, allowing borrowers with varying credit and lengthy approval processes associated with profiles and financial backgrounds to access funds. This traditional lenders. The efficiency of the P2P lending opens up opportunities for individuals who may not process allows borrowers to access funds quickly, qualify for loans from traditional institutions to obtain making it particularly advantageous for individuals who the financing they need for various purposes, such as require prompt financing. The digital nature of peer-to-debt consolidation, starting a business, or funding peer lending platforms also enables borrowers to personal projects.

conveniently track their loan status, make payments, and communicate with lenders through the platform's Peer-to-peer lending can offer borrowers competitive interface.

interest rates compared to traditional lenders. With P2P lending, interest rates are often determined Peer-to-peer lending fosters a sense of community and through a bidding process where lenders compete to connection between borrowers and lenders. Unlike fund loans by offering lower interest rates. This traditional lending, where borrowers have limited marketplace dynamic can lead to more favorable rates knowledge about the lenders, P2P lending platforms for borrowers, especially those with good credit histories often encourage communication and interaction.

and attractive loan proposals. The absence of traditional Borrowers can share their stories, goals, and reasons for banking overheads and intermediaries also contributes seeking financing, while lenders can learn about the to potentially lower interest rates. As a result, borrowers individuals or businesses they are supporting. This may be able to save money on interest payments over transparency and personal connection can create a the life of their loans.

unique lending experience, where borrowers feel supported by a community of individuals who believe in Peer-to-peer lending presents an appealing investment their ventures. For lenders, it provides an opportunity to option for individuals looking to diversify their directly contribute to the success of others, building a investment portfolio. Lenders on P2P lending platforms sense of fulfillment and potentially forming long-term have the opportunity to allocate their funds across relationships with borrowers.

multiple loans, thereby spreading their risk. By investing in different loans with varying risk profiles, Peer-to-peer lending offers a range of benefits, including lenders can reduce their exposure to any single a streamlined application process, efficient approval borrower. Additionally, lenders have the potential to timelines, the opportunity to build relationships within a earn attractive returns on their investments through lending community, and the convenience of digital interest payments made by borrowers. P2P lending platforms. These advantages have contributed to the offers a way for individuals to participate in the lending growth and popularity of P2P lending as an alternative market and potentially generate passive income while financing option for both borrowers and lenders.

supporting others in fulfilling their financial needs.

However, as with any financial activity, it's important for borrowers and lenders to carefully assess the risks and consider their individual circumstances before participating in peer-to-peer lending activities.

PEER-TO-PEER LENDING

How to Choose a Lending Platform

Before choosing a peer-to-peer lending platform, conduct thorough research and assess the platform's reputation. Look for established platforms with a solid track record and positive reviews from borrowers and lenders. Check for any red flags, such as negative customer feedback, regulatory issues, or unresolved complaints. Consider platforms that have been operating for a considerable period and have successfully facilitated a significant number of loan transactions. Reliable platforms are more likely to have robust security measures, clear policies, and efficient dispute resolution processes, ensuring a trustworthy and safe lending environment.

Evaluate the loan diversity and borrower profiles available on the platform. A diverse range of loan types and purposes indicates a healthy marketplace and can provide more opportunities for lenders. Look for platforms that offer loans across different categories such as personal loans, small business loans, education loans, or real estate loans. Assess the borrower profiles to ensure there is a mix of creditworthy individuals or businesses seeking financing. A platform with a variety of loan options and borrowers increases the likelihood of finding suitable lending opportunities that align with your investment goals and risk tolerance.

Consider the platform features and user experience offered by the peer-to-peer lending platform.

Evaluate the platform's user interface, functionality, and ease of use. Look for platforms that provide Pay attention to the level of transparency and security comprehensive loan information, borrower profiles, provided by the peer-to-peer lending platform. Transparency and transparent interest rates. User-friendly features includes clear and comprehensive information about the such as filtering options, loan performance data, and lending process, fees, and potential risks involved. Look for automated investing tools can enhance the overall platforms that disclose the terms, conditions, and potential fees experience for lenders. Additionally, consider the upfront, ensuring you have a complete understanding of the platform's customer support and responsiveness.

lending arrangement. Assess the platform's security measures to protect both borrowers' and lenders' sensitive information.

Efficient customer support can be crucial when you Encryption protocols, data privacy policies, and robust need assistance or have questions regarding your authentication processes are essential features to look for in a lending activities. A well-designed platform with trustworthy platform. A transparent and secure platform gives intuitive features and excellent user experience can lenders confidence in participating and safeguards their contribute to a smooth and satisfying lending interests throughout the lending journey.

experience.

Considering research and reputation, loan diversity and borrower profiles, platform features and user experience, as well as transparency and security, will help you choose a peer-to-peer lending platform that aligns with your lending goals, risk tolerance, and overall preferences. By selecting a reliable and user-friendly platform, you can enhance your lending experience and maximize the potential benefits of participating in peer-to-peer lending.

PEER-TO-PEER LENDING

Risks & Chal enges

Unlike traditional lenders who often require collateral to One of the primary risks in peer-to-peer lending is the secure loans, peer-to-peer lending typically operates without potential for borrowers to default on their loans. While collateral. This lack of physical assets as security poses a risk to platforms often conduct credit assessments and assign risk lenders. In the event of borrower default, lenders may have ratings to borrowers, there is still a degree of uncertainty limited recourse to recover their investments. While platforms involved. Lenders may encounter situations where borrowers may have collection processes in place, the effectiveness of are unable to repay their loans due to financial difficulties, these processes can vary, and the recovery of funds may be changing circumstances, or other reasons. This default risk challenging. Additionally, the absence of collateral increases can result in the loss of the principal amount invested by the vulnerability to fraudulent activities, as borrowers may lenders. It is important for lenders to diversify their lending misrepresent their financial information or intentions. Lenders portfolios and carefully assess the creditworthiness of should carefully assess the credibility and reliability of borrowers before committing funds to minimize the impact of borrowers, rely on proper documentation, and consider the potential defaults.

potential impact of loan defaults on their overall lending portfolio.

Peer-to-peer lending platforms themselves can present risks and challenges. Some platforms may not have a long track record or established reputation, which could raise concerns Lenders participating in peer-to-peer lending should about their stability and reliability. There is a possibility of carefully evaluate the credit and default risk associated platform failure or closure, which can lead to loss of funds or with borrowers, diversify their lending portfolios, and disruptions in loan servicing. Additionally, regulatory conduct thorough due diligence. They should also considerations vary across different jurisdictions, and consider the platform risk, ensuring the platform is platforms must comply with relevant laws and regulations.

reputable, secure, and compliant with regulatory Changes in regulatory frameworks or legal requirements requirements. By understanding and mitigating these could impact the operations and viability of peer-to-peer risks, lenders can make informed decisions and navigate lending platforms. Lenders should be aware of the regulatory landscape and assess the platform's compliance measures and the challenges associated with peer-to-peer lending adherence to industry best practices.

effectively.

"Challenges are what make life interesting and overcoming them is what makes life

meaningful." - Joshua J. Marine

PEER-TO-PEER LENDING

Tips for Succes

In the world of peer-to-peer (P2P) lending, understanding the risk and reward balance is crucial. Every loan carries a degree of risk -

borrowers can default, and if they do, you may lose your investment. Platforms often provide risk ratings for borrowers, which can guide you in your investment choices. Generally, higher risk loans offer higher potential returns, but also carry a higher chance of default. Therefore, diversifying your investment across different risk levels can help balance potential returns with manageable risk.

Diversification is a fundamental principle of investing that applies strongly to P2P lending.

The key is to invest small amounts in many different loans, rather than a large amount in a few. This way, if a borrower defaults on their loan, only a small portion of your investment is impacted. Some platforms even offer automatic diversification tools, which can simplify this process and help protect your investment.

Just as important as diversification is the careful analysis of borrower profiles. P2P platforms provide data about each potential borrower, including credit scores, loan purpose, and sometimes more personal details. By taking the time to understand who you're lending to, you can make more informed decisions and choose investments that align with your comfort level in P2P lending platforms and regulations can

terms of risk.

change over time, and it's important to stay updated about these changes. Regularly

One of the keys to growing wealth is to reinvest check in on your investments, keep an eye

returns, and the same holds true in P2P lending.

on the performance of your loans, and When you receive payments from borrowers, these should be reinvested into new loans. This watch for news or updates from your P2P

allows you to compound your returns over time, platform. Staying informed will help you thereby maximizing your overall earnings. Some adjust your strategy as needed and optimize platforms offer automatic reinvestment features, your returns over time.

which can make this process easier.

CREATING A RENTAL BUSINESS

What is a Rental Busines ?

A rental business is an entrepreneurial venture that involves leasing or renting out assets or properties to There are many variations and opportunities in clients or customers over a specified period. These the rental business landscape. Some businesses, assets could range from physical properties like like real estate rentals, operate on longer-term houses, apartments, and commercial buildings, to contracts and provide a steady, predictable movable properties like cars, equipment, and income stream. Others, like event equipment machinery, to intangible properties like software or rentals, may have shorter rental periods and digital content. The rental business model is based on the premise that not everyone who needs access to a fluctuating demand. Technological

certain asset can afford or wants to own it advancements have also led to the rise of online permanently, and would prefer to rent it for a rental businesses, like peer-to-peer property specific duration instead.

rentals and digital content subscriptions.

Despite the type of rental business, the core idea The operational structure of a rental business remains the same: providing temporary access to involves acquiring assets and maintaining them to assets for a fee, thereby creating a sustainable ensure they are in a rentable condition. The business source of income.

then markets these assets to potential renters, sets rental terms and conditions, and collects rent over the agreed period. A rental business earns income through the fees charged to the renters, usually calculated as a fixed amount per day, week, month, or year, depending on the nature of the asset and the market conditions.

RENTAL BUSINESS

According to a report from the Joint Center for Housing Studies of Harvard University, in the United States alone, the number of renter Benefits of Creating

households surpassed 43 million in 2019.

a Rental Busines

One of the primary benefits of a rental There can be tax benefits associated with business is the steady and predictable cash running a rental business. Depending on the flow it can generate. By renting out assets, laws in your country or region, you may be able whether they are real estate properties, to deduct business expenses, including

equipment, or other goods, you can establish a maintenance, repair costs, and depreciation, reliable stream of income. Regular rental from your taxable income. These benefits can payments can provide stability that other significantly reduce your tax burden and business models may not offer. In the case of increase the overall profitability of your property rentals, for example, once a tenant business. Always consult with a tax signs a lease, you can count on receiving a set professional to understand the potential tax amount of income for the duration of that benefits and obligations for your specific lease.

situation.

In addition to rental income, a rental business Finally, a rental business can offer a high may also benefit from asset appreciation, degree of flexibility and control. As the owner, especially in the real estate sector. Over time, you can make decisions about the assets you assets like property often increase in value.

invest in, how much you charge for rent, and While this isn't income in the liquid sense how you manage and maintain your assets.

until you sell the property, it represents This control extends to choosing when and growing equity and wealth. This financial where you work, making a rental business a growth can serve as a safety net or a source of potentially good fit for entrepreneurs seeking a capital for future investments.

flexible lifestyle. This flexibility, combined with the financial benefits, can make a rental Rental businesses can often scale up relatively business a rewarding venture.

easily, which is another significant advantage.

Once you have a successful model for

acquiring and renting out a particular type of asset, you can repeat that model with additional assets. This allows your business to grow and increase its income over time. The scalability can also be geographic, with the potential to expand your rental business to new locations.

RENTAL BUSINESS

Types of Rental Busines es

Real Estate Rental Business

Real estate rental businesses are among the most common types of rental ventures. They involve renting out residential properties, such as apartments, houses, or vacation homes, to individuals or families. Commercial real estate rentals are another branch, where properties like office spaces, retail stores, or warehouses are leased to businesses. This type of rental business can provide a steady income stream, especially with long-term tenants, and the potential for property appreciation over time.

Vehicle Rental Business

Vehicle rental businesses cater to people who need temporary use of a vehicle. This category includes car rental companies that offer vehicles for short periods, often to travelers or individuals whose own vehicles are temporarily unavailable. It can also include more specialized vehicle rentals, such as RVs, motorcycles, or luxury cars. Some businesses focus on leasing commercial vehicles, like trucks or vans, to other businesses.

Equipment Rental Business

Equipment rental businesses provide temporary access to various types of equipment. This can range from construction equipment, like excavators and bulldozers, to event necessities, like audio-visual equipment or party supplies. Businesses and individuals often prefer to rent equipment for a specific job or event rather than investing in owning, storing, and maintaining it themselves. This creates a lucrative market for equipment rental companies.

Online Rental Business

The rise of the digital economy has seen a growth in online rental businesses. These businesses leverage technology to connect asset owners with potential renters. Examples include peer-to-peer property rentals, such as Airbnb, or fashion rentals, like Rent the Runway. Digital content can also be rented online, with businesses like Netflix or Spotify offering streaming services for movies, TV shows, or music.

"Financial freedom is less

Specialty Rental Business

about financials and more

Specialty rental businesses focus on niche markets with specific needs. This could include renting out high-end cameras and about freedom."

lenses to photographers, musical instruments to musicians, or sports equipment to enthusiasts. Another example is the luxury

- Manoj Arora

boat or yacht rental business, catering to vacationers or event planners. These businesses succeed by understanding their niche market's unique needs and providing high-quality, reliable rental services.

RENTAL BUSINESS

Risks & Chal enges

The most immediate risk in starting a rental business is financial. Purchasing properties or assets to rent out requires a significant upfront investment. Moreover, there can be

ongoing costs for maintenance, repairs, insurance,

and

possibly

property

management. If the rental income does not

cover these costs or if the properties sit vacant for extended periods, the business could face financial strain or even failure.

Rental businesses are subject to market volatility. Economic downturns can decrease demand for rentals or affect the ability of tenants to pay their rent. In the real estate sector, property values can fluctuate,

impacting the value of your investment.

Similarly, in the equipment rental sector, demand can vary based on industry trends and economic conditions. Staying abreast of market trends and being prepared to adapt

is critical in managing this risk.

Rental businesses must navigate a range of regulatory challenges. These can include zoning laws for property rentals, safety regulations for equipment rentals, and

licensing requirements for certain types of Lastly, the assets in a rental business can rental businesses. Non-compliance can result depreciate over time or become obsolete. This in fines, legal action, or business closure. It's is particularly true in sectors like technology or crucial to understand and adhere to all machinery rentals, where new models relevant regulations in your jurisdiction.

frequently come onto the market. Maintaining and updating your rental assets to remain Working with tenants or renters presents its competitive can be a significant ongoing cost.

own set of challenges. You may encounter Similarly, real estate properties require regular tenants who fail to pay rent on time, damage maintenance and occasional renovations to the property, or violate the terms of their retain their value and appeal to renters.

lease. Dealing with these issues can be time- Despite these risks and challenges, many rental consuming and costly. In some cases, you businesses thrive by carefully managing these may need to engage in legal proceedings to potential pitfalls, conducting thorough market evict a problematic tenant or recover unpaid research, and providing excellent service to rent.

their renters.

CONCLUSION

Achieve Financial Fre dom

Passive income, often lauded as the key to financial freedom, is income that requires little to no effort to earn and maintain. It's the dream of earning money while you sleep, or while you travel the world, that makes passive income so appealing. Unlike a traditional job where you trade hours for dollars, passive income strategies can generate returns 24/7, regardless of whether you're working, relaxing, or even sleeping. This allows you to break free from the confines of an hourly wage and begin building wealth on your terms.

Financial freedom is the point where your passive income can cover your living expenses.

It's about having your financial resources providing for your life and lifestyle, rather than you providing for them. When you achieve this state, you're no longer tethered to a job or employer for survival. You have the

independence to pursue what truly matters to you, whether that's more family time, travel, a passion project, or even a career shift into something you love but were afraid didn't pay enough.

Anyone can start building passive income, but it doesn't happen overnight. It takes time, effort, and sometimes, a bit of upfront investment. The first step is to choose a passive income strategy that aligns with your interests and skills. This The journey to financial freedom begins with a could be investing in stocks or bonds, starting a single step. Start today by exploring passive rental business, creating an online course, income strategies and choosing one to focus on.

writing a book, or even starting a blog or Remember, the goal isn't to create immediate YouTube channel. It's important to remember wealth, but to build sustainable income streams that while these strategies can eventually generate passive income, they often require that will continue to pay off in the future.

significant initial effort to set up.

Don't wait for the perfect moment – start now.

Every day you delay is a day of potential Building passive income is a journey that passive income lost. Take the first step towards requires persistence and patience. There may be your financial freedom today, and open the setbacks along the way, and your passive income door to a future where you control your time, streams might take time to mature. But by your life, and your wealth.

staying committed, continuously learning, and adapting your strategies as needed, you can gradually increase your passive income and move closer to financial freedom.

www.ingramcontent.com/pod-product-compliance
Lightning Source LLC
Chambersburg PA
CBHW070451220526
45466CB00004B/1801